Creative Mindfulness

Buddha-Inspired Tips for Writers and Artists

Table of Contents

Chapter 1. Introduction

Unlock the tranquility of your creative soul with our Special Report on "Creative Mindfulness: Buddha-Inspired Tips for Writers and Artists". Amidst a world storming with distractions, our captivating report offers a serene escape to help rekindle the inventive spark that exists within you, all drawing upon the profound wisdom of Buddha. Motivating stories, meaningful tips, enlightening exercises - we've lovingly curated beautiful paths to cradle your creativity and nurture your sense of mindfulness. Even as you read this, feel the excitement brewing within; for you're one step closer to transforming your artistic journey into a remarkably mindful quest. Say 'Yes' today to a blissful blend of serenity and creation that can genuinely propel your artistic journey towards uncharted horizons! Purchase our Special Report now, and let's embark on this awe-inspiring journey together!

Chapter 2. Unlocking the Power of Mindful Creation

Our creative journey often feels like exploring an unfamiliar landscape. We are both the traveller and the cartographer, detailing the richness of our experiences while simultaneously shaping our pathways. The wisdom of Buddha offers us a profound map, leading us towards the gate of 'mindful creation'. Instilling this mindfulness into our creative process instigates the unlocking of new perspectives and reignites the spark of creativity that rests, ever-patient, within our souls.

2.1. Understanding Mindful Creation

Mindfulness, a state of purposeful and present awareness, seemingly takes birth an ocean away from the frenetic shores of creativity and imagination. However, when entwined, the practice of mindfulness and creativity form a remarkable tapestry, generating what we now understand as 'Mindful Creation'.

As we dive into the clarity of the present moment during mindfulness practices, we find ourselves encountering our thoughts and emotions more vividly. In this space of heightened awareness and with an open mind, the veil of subconscious coverings lifts to expose our most potent creative source. Witnessing our thoughts without judgement or attachment allows us to tap into this reservoir and channel its vibrant hues into our canvas of creativity.

2.2. Mindfulness: A Bridge between Inner and Outer Worlds

Buddha taught that the key to understanding our universe lies within. To tap into the universe of creativity, we must first learn to venture inward—into the self. Mindfulness serves as a sturdy, yet gentle, bridge connecting our inner self with the outer world. It's a bridge constructed not of bricks and mortar but of attentiveness, acceptance, and understanding. As we traverse this causeway, the intricate patterns of our thoughts and emotions rise into lucidity, providing fodder for our creative machinery.

2.3. Unveiling Creativity through Awareness and Acceptance

The act of creativity is far more than a collection of rhythmic words, vivid colors, or melodious notes. At its core, creativity is a process of self-exploration and self-expression. It is interwoven with who we 'are', what we 'experience', and how we 'perceive'. Aware of these relations, the conscious, non-judgemental awareness cultivated through mindfulness integrates organically with the creative process.

In practicing mindful creation, we allow ourselves to reduce our reactivity to emotions and thoughts that often stunt our creative energy. Learning to accept these interior landscapes—instead of refuting or avoiding negative feelings—we encourage the transformation of these very thoughts and emotions into nourishment for our creative spirit.

2.4. The Art of Cultivating Mindful Creation

There are several ways we can effectively infuse mindfulness into our creative journey. Here we explore a few:

1. Begin with a Mindful Pause: Before launching into the creative process, take a moment to ground yourself in the present moment. This practice can involve nothing more complex than a few, slow breaths. The difference between ordinary breathing and a mindful breath lies within the awareness.

2. Create a Mindful Space: Just as a garden needs fertile soil to flourish, creativity needs a nurturing environment to bloom. A physical space uncluttered and inviting can help create a mental environment conducive to productivity and inventiveness.

3. Practice Mindful Observation: Once in your mindful space, practice observation without judgement. Observe your thoughts, emotions, ideas and inspirations. At times, even the raw materials of your creation—such as words, colors, or sounds—benefit from such unbiased examination.

4. Cultivate Mindful Listening: Spending time in silence, listening to the orchestration of our surrounding world, or the silent gush of our thoughts, can help refuel our creative energy.

With these methods in your creative toolbox, peaceful presence and creative exploration become harmoniously aligned, enhancing the richness and depth of your work.

2.5. Embracing Mindful Creation: A Step Towards Blissful Artistic Expression

As you open the doors of your creative mind to the possibilities of mindful creation, a blissful journey of artistic exploration awaits. Far from being a hindrance, mindfulness can aid in releasing our fears, biases, and self-judgement, allowing creativity to flow unimpeded, like a river free of debris.

Undeniably, embarking on the path of mindful creation proposes a unique exploration of self and artistry. Yet, remember, the path is not always a straight road; it winds and meanders, much like the creative process itself. However, this journey is not one you undertake alone—it is a collective experience, shared by creatives seeking to unlock extraordinary potential.

Grounded in Buddha's wisdom, the power of mindful creation awaits you, poised on the brink of realization. Embrace it—dive deep into the vivid landscapes of your soul and paint your world with the tranquil colors of mindfulness. The beauty will astound you. Your art, born of mindful creation, will inspire others. And together, we shall redefine what it means to create.

Chapter 3. Buddha-Inspired Mindfulness for Artists: The Basics

The journey into creativity begins not with a brush or a pen, but within the calm corners of our minds. Let's explore this journey together.

3.1. Understanding Mindfulness, The Buddha Way

The Buddha taught about the balance between mindfulness (Sati) and clear comprehension (Sampajañña). Mindfulness is being fully present in the moment, completely aware, not thinking about the past, not dreaming about the future, but just being. Clear comprehension refers to understanding and discerning the ongoing experience in that present moment.

When we are mindful, we observe our life from a distance. We don't judge whether the things happening are good or bad. We simply acknowledge them, stay relaxed, and move forward. The essence of mindfulness is to be awake and aware, observing life as it unfolds.

3.2. Embracing the Present Moment

One of the essential teachings of Buddha is about the importance of being present. Creativity blossoms when we are no longer slaves of our past or future. When a creator starts cherishing the now, every stroke they paint, every word they write carries a bit of themselves, a part of their present moment, making their creation more authentic and powerful.

Moreover, staying present also implies making friends with solitude. Only in moments of solitude can we confront our thoughts, observe them, understand them, and transform them into a creative expression.

3.3. The Four Foundations of Mindfulness

Buddha talked about the Four Foundations of Mindfulness, a profound practice for training the mind. We can leverage this practice to become better artists and writers.

1. **Mindfulness of the body (Kayanupassana)**: As creators, we need to be fully aware of our bodily sensations. It helps us understand our bodily responses to different stimuli and influence our art accordingly.

2. **Mindfulness of feelings (Vedananupassana)**: As emotional beings, our feelings give life to our art and writing. By being mindful of our emotions, we can channel them into our work, making it more relatable and profound.

3. **Mindfulness of mind (Cittanupassana)**: This involves understanding our mental states, our thoughts, and biases. It helps us to avoid overthinking and worrying, letting the creativity to flow naturally.

4. **Mindfulness of mental phenomena (Dhammanupassana)**: This involves observing how our mind reacts to different experiences. Understanding these responses helps us add depth to our creative expressions.

3.4. Buddha-Inspired Practices for Mindful Creativity

Several Buddha-inspired practices can intensify your creative endeavours. Let's delve deeper into them:

- *Sati (Mindfulness):* Develop a habit of being observant. Whether you're washing dishes, walking in the park, or simply breathing, be completely there, in the moment. This habit of presence will reflect in your creative work too.

- *Metta (Loving-kindness):* Buddha stressed the importance of loving-kindness and compassion. As creators, enveloping ourselves and our creative process with Metta can lead to work filled with love and understanding.

- *Samadhi (Meditative Absorption):* Daily meditation can propel your creativity by enhancing your connection with yourself, the ultimate source of your creativity.

- *Vipassana (Insight):* A practice of self-observation, it helps us understand our thoughts deeply and let the wisdom from within flow into our creation.

3.5. Incorporating Mindful Practices into Your Creative Routine

Finally, it's important to talk about implementing these practices into the daily routine. Here is a step-by-step guide:

1. *Morning Meditation:* Begin your day with a meditation session of at least 15 minutes. You will find deep peace and comfort in this silent communication with yourself.

2. *Mindful Journaling:* Maintain a journal where you can document your thoughts, emotions, and dreams. It not only declutters your

mind but also becomes a rich source of inspiration for your creative work.

3. *Nature Walks:* Spend time with nature, observe its calm, its chaos, colors, and moods. Such exposure to the raw beauty will likely spark your creative energy.

4. *Artist Dates:* Set aside a day or time in a week where you can pursue activities distinctively different from your usual art practice. It starts to hone your creative instincts and makes you more observant.

5. *Gratitude Practice:* Before bedtime, reflect on your day, acknowledge the moments that brought you peace, and express gratitude for them privately. It generates a positive mindset, proactively boosting your creativity.

In a world overwhelmed with distractions, the greatest tool an artist or writer can possess is a mind at peace and brimming with awareness. Every crumpled paper or stained canvas is not a failure, but a stepping stone to something even greater. It is this serenity and acceptance we aim to foster within you. Taking this path may not always be smooth, but the rewards in terms of your creative development can be plentiful and beautifully transformative.

Adopting mindfulness practices will not only imbue your creations with a unique charm but you as a creator will experience a state of peace, bliss, and fulfillment that goes beyond the realm of words and colors.

Chapter 4. Writing in the Flow: The Buddhist Approach

The act of creating art, be it through words, paints, or music, is often believed to transcend the boundaries of the conscious mind and to flirt with the ethereal world. It implies an immersive state, aptly called the 'flow state', a term originally coined by the psychologist Mihaly Csikszentmihalyi. In the eyes of Buddhism, this flow state is where mindfulness lies, creating a bridge to our true selves and the purity of the process.

4.1. Embracing the Ways of Buddha

Understanding the Buddhist perspective involves embracing the 'Middle Way', which with respect to writing and artistry holds the idea that neither extreme self-indulgence nor self-mortification will lead to creative enlightenment. Instead, a balance between the two, abiding by principles of mindfulness, will help us reach artistic nirvana.

Buddha teaches us to pay keen attention to the present moment and to release ourselves from the grasp of past regrets or future worries. This primary Buddhist notion gracefully weaves itself into the art of writing and creating. When you write or create in the present, guided not by judgements but by conscious awareness, you connect with the truth of life and give birth to authentic art.

4.2. The Art of Awareness

Mindfulness promotes acute awareness of your thoughts, your surroundings, your body, and your soul. This understanding can then channelize into the transmutation of these aspects into your art or writing.

To fill your creative cup with the clear water of consciousness, adopt simple practices like meditation or focused breathing. When you complete these practices before your writing or artistry sessions, you ground yourself in awareness. Watch as your pen begins to dance, mirroring the rhythm of your measured breaths, and the echo of your beating heart.

4.3. The Tenet of Impermanence

Another profound principle that Buddha imparted was the concept of 'Anicca' or 'Impermanence.' It suggests the transient nature of all phenomena, emotions, situations, and life itself. In the context of writing or artistry, this principle reminds you that every creative block or hard phase is impermanent too. It's merely an ephemeral cloud that overshadows your luminous creative sun. Impermanence also suggests the ever-evolving nature of your creativity – it's boundless, ever-growing, always changing - hence, embracing this can open up one's mind to vast realms of possibilities.

4.4. The Middle Way in Writing

Akin to the Buddhist Middle Path, maintaining a balance in your writing style is equally essential. Avoid literary self-indulgence, where complex jargon overshadows the crux of the message. Concurrently, resist self-mortification, where underselling your ideas due to fear of judgment or repression results in insipid written works. Strive for simplicity, clarity, and authenticity, using language as the vessel to communicate and connect without losing your unique voice.

Incorporating the Middle Way's practices can contribute to a healthier, more positive creative process that ensures artistic longevity. This framework reminds you that your artistic journey isn't linear but cyclical, much like the Buddhist belief in birth, death, and rebirth. There will be progress, delay, enlightenment, confusion, but at the core of it, an unwavering and relentless passion for creation.

4.5. The Sphere of Mindful Creating

As we delve deeper into Buddhist-inspired methods, it's significant to note that to achieve a state of 'flow' in writing or creating, we cover three main dimensions:

1. Conscious observation - Immerse yourself in the ongoing moment, observing every little emotion, thought, environmental detail, and sensory experience.

2. Uninterrupted creation - Engage in writing or creating without disruptions, not letting external or internal interventions hinder the process.

3. Detached evaluation - Evaluate your work as a separate entity, almost as if it's not your creation.

When these three dimensions come together, they forge an amalgamation of mindfulness and creativity that can truly transform one's artistic journey.

4.6. Struggles into Strengths: An Anecdote

Many renowned creators have faced bouts of pain, despair, and depression, but the true artists are those who mindfully turn these struggles into strengths. Turning to Buddhism, we find inspiring stories, such as that of Milarepa, a Tibetan yogi and poet who dealt with enormous guilt and regret for his earlier crimes. However, through arduous meditation and soulful songwriting, he transmuted his guilt into the highest form of enlightenment.

This narrative indeed serves as a potent reminder of the power of mindful creation. It reinforces the idea that regardless of the nature of our past or present circumstances, through self-awareness, self-compassion, and self-evolution, we can extract meaningful stories and heart-touching art.

Our pursuit of creativity, aided with the soothing tenets of Buddha, can not only enhance the quality of our art but also the quality of our lives. By fostering mindfulness, we can untie the knots of our subconscious and clear the creative blockades, thus opening the floodgates of boundless imagination. Here, every moment stretches into a cosmic canvas upon which we can paint with our thoughts, emotions, and stories.

In the grand scheme of things, remember that your creative journey should never be a sprint but a wonderfully serene pilgrimage, every step of which is a testament to the marriage of mindfulness and creativity. As Buddha wisely put it, "It is better to travel well than to arrive."

Chapter 5. Examining the Buddha's Teachings for Enhanced Creativity

Our creative journey unveils a layered landscape of emotions, ideas and expressions. It is essential to navigate this landscape with mindful precision and awaken to the profound teachings of Buddha. Let's see how these serene teachings can transcend your creativity to a realm of enlightenment.

5.1. Delving into Buddha's Wisdom

To truly understand the junction of creativity and mindfulness, we must plunge into the Buddha's wisdom. Buddha emphasized the importance of Four Noble Truths and The Eightfold Path that channel understanding and empathy. Let's delve deep into the essence of these teachings.

The First Noble Truth: Life is abundant with suffering, and it's an essential part of existence. Counterintuitively, artists find their fuel in turbulence and hardships. The acknowledgment of suffering helps to create a connection with your work, making it more authentic.

The Second Noble Truth: The root cause of suffering is our desires and attachments. An artist should be conscious of attachments towards certain ideas or creative processes. This sense of detachment can lead to a more diversified creative path.

The Third Noble Truth: Letting go of attachments will cease the suffering. Releasing your creative expectations allows for the free flow of innovation and expressions.

The Fourth Noble Truth: Following the Eightfold Path is the way towards cessation of suffering. By incorporating the elements of this path into your creative process, you can enhance mindfulness and creativity.

5.2. The Eightfold Path to Creative Enlightenment

The Eightfold Path describes the way out of suffering and towards self-loving liberation. Let's explore how each step can be intertwined into our creative processes.

Right Understanding: To channel your creative energy, it's crucial to have a realistic and deeper understanding of your art. This clarity aids in constructing purposeful artwork.

Right Thought: Thoughts determine your actions. Cultivate positive thought process to help your creativity bloom.

Right Speech: In creative processes, "Right Speech" means to constructively criticize one's work. Avoid harsh judgments and appreciate the process.

Right Action: Create art responsibly. It should contribute positively towards the viewers and the society.

Right Livelihood: Ensure that your creativity shapes an ethical career. It should not only financially sustain you, but also cultivate a sense of fulfillment.

Right Effort: Consistent effort is vital for creativity. Strive to put wholehearted effort into every piece of work.

Right Mindfulness: Engage completely with your work. Minimize the distractions and immerse yourself into the art.

Right Concentration: Harness the power of deep focus. Concentration forms an integral part of the artistic process.

5.3. Mindful Practices To Boost Creativity

Creativity thrives when the mind is calm and the soul, serene. Buddha's teachings inspire the following practices that can drive creativity to new heights.

Meditation: Regular mindfulness meditation enhances focus and fosters novel ideas. It cultivates a mind-space that's receptive to fresh perspectives.

Loving-kindness: Developing the practice of metta, or loving-kindness, can bring forth compassionate energy in your art, making it more relatable and profound.

Mindful Walking: This simple practice of walking mindfully helps us stay grounded, bringing clarity and calmness into our creative endeavours.

5.4. Lessons from Buddha's Life

Buddha's life was in itself a narrative of ultimate liberation. His experiences teach us many valuable lessons applicable in a creative scenario.

Overcoming Fear: Fear stymies creativity. Buddha's journey of attaining enlightenment, despite his fear of change, reassures us that fear can be conquered.

Transforming Anguish into Positivity: Buddha used his suffering as a tool to find enlightenment. Similarly, we should use our struggles as a transformative energy to create intense, personal art.

Coexistence: Buddha's teachings promote unity and connectivity with all beings. Our art should echo these principles, delivering a profound message of unity.

Let this philosophical blend of mindfulness and creativity be your guiding light. Dive deep into the vast ocean of your potential, swim across the currents of ideas, and emerge, artistically enlightened. Enjoy the journey, for the Buddhist-inspired artistic path is as enriching as the creative outcome. Unleash the calm within the chaos. Breathe life into your creations. For, as Buddha once claimed, "Your work is to discover your world and then with all your heart give yourself to it."

Chapter 6. Artistry and Compassion: The Intersection

Artistry and compassion are two threads that often weave together the tapestry of creativity. They are interconnected, both contributing to mindfulness and indeed, to the Buddha-inspired path of creation we are exploring.

6.1. The Connection Between Artistry and Compassion

Artistry is the creative soul's expression, a way of crafting images, rhythms, stories, melodies, and more that represent experiences, dreams, or perspectives. Simultaneously, compassion is a profound empathy, a sense of caring that embraces understanding, kindness, and a deep connection with others.

These two elements, when combined, form a powerful conduit for creative mindfulness. The artist or writer who engages deeply with compassion often finds untapped wells of inventiveness, pathos, and inspiration. The compassionate individual who delves into artistry often discovers fresh ways of expressing kindness, unity, and understanding.

In each artistic endeavor, be it a painting or a prose, a symphony or a sculpture, compassion can serve to deepen the impact, expand the audience's understanding, and enhance the artist's satisfaction. As Buddha wisely articulated, "Compassion is that which makes the heart of the good move at the pain of others. It crushes and destroys the pain of others. Thus, it is called compassion. It is called compassion because it shelters and embraces the distressed."

6.2. Compassionate Creativity: The Buddha's Principles

The Buddha had a profound understanding of compassion that translates well to the creative process. He urged his followers to cultivate a deep sense of empathy for all fellow beings, a practice that can also serve creative endeavors wonderfully.

An artist who leans into compassionate creativity often finds their work more resonant, more profound, and more universally appealing. A writer who infuses their prose with a sense of understanding and kindness will likely see their readers more engaged and impacted.

The Buddha's principles of ethical conduct - or sila, meditation - or samadhi, and wisdom - or pañña, form the fundamental components of the Eightfold Path, which holds incredible relevance for artists who dare to integrate compassion into their creative process.

===Silence and Observation

Silence is not just an absence of noise but a clarity of mind that can stimulate an artist's imagination. It is in the stillness of silence that artists can turn inwards, introspecting, observing their thoughts, and drawing inferences that take shape as their artistic expressions.

===Empathy in Action

One cannot fully grasp the depth of another's experience through observation alone. Actively practicing empathy contributes to a deep and nuanced understanding, one that breeds genuine connections. This emotional investment can be mirrored back in artistic representations, resonating with an audience by touching their hearts and sparking mutual understanding.

===The Liberation of Compassion

By detaching oneself from the confines of ego, an artist can perceive their environment from a perspective free from judgment and prejudices. This liberation elevates consciousness and lets compassion guide the process of creation, resulting in art that truly reflects the human spirit and experience.

Artists' work, touched by compassion, can go beyond the realm of self-expression. Their creations can act as a mirror to society, a catalyst for change, a bridge between hearts, an inspiration for action, and a testament to universal human experience.

6.3. The Compassionate Artist: Lessons From Buddha

Compassion is not merely a personal trait. It's a dynamic, vital force that can form the philosophical backbone of an artist's work. The Buddhist perspective, steeped in understanding, wisdom, and empathy lends artists an enriched point of creative departure.

Translating the Buddha's teachings into practical exercises for artists, we find inspiration, motivation, and of course, compassion - elements that let artists transform their creative journey into a mindful quest.

1. **Meditation and Mindfulness:** Immersion in artistic work is akin to a meditative state. Practicing mindfulness allows artists to be fully present in each moment, experiencing emotions and inspiration as they flow. This heightened sense of awareness can deepen the artist's connection with their work.

2. **Understanding the Transient Nature of Life:** Comprehending the concept of impermanence can give your work a profound depth. Life is not constant, and neither is art. Embracing this idea can open up avenues for growth and exploration in your artwork.

3. **Practicing Detachment:** Arts, like life, are journey-driven, not

destination-driven. The value lies in the process, not only in the end result. Internalizing this attitude will draw you deeper into your art, enhancing its power and authenticity.

4. **Empowering Through Art:** Art holds the power to uplift and heal. Through compassionate works, you can speak volumes, serve humanity, and inspire change. Your art can become a voice for the voiceless, a beacon of hope, a testament to resilience.

By nurturing empathy and endorsing love and unity in their work, artists not only enhance their creativity but also contribute positively to the world. Through the eyes of compassion, art transforms from a solitary endeavor into a collective experience. This intersection is where artistry and compassion truly bloom, fostering an environment conducive to mindful creation, enriched ideas, and soulful satisfaction. Let's continue this enthralling journey, fusing creativity and compassion, as we venture onwards and delve deeper into creative mindfulness.

Chapter 7. Mindfulness Techniques to Boost Artistic Focus

An artistic journey is punctuated with both moments of great inspiration and periods of intense struggle. Our creativity can seemingly ebb and flow with the circumstances of our lives, making it sometimes difficult to stay focused on the art we love. Employing mindfulness techniques allows us to channel our attention back to our craft. Let us explore these techniques in depth.

7.1. Embrace the Present

The first step in boosting your artistic focus through mindfulness is to train yourself to be fully present in the current moment. This practice, highly promoted by Buddha, is crucial in eliminating distractions and increasing productivity.

Start by sitting in a quiet place before your work. This could be your desk, studio, or a corner in your park—anywhere that allows you to feel comfortable and tranquil. Close your eyes, and for a few moments, breathe in and out, focusing on the air entering your nostrils and escaping your mouth. This technique helps ground you in the present moment, setting aside the distractions of past regrets and future worries, directing your entire attention to the task at hand.

7.2. Establish a Mindfulness Routine

Inculcating a routine promotes discipline, which in turn supports and nurtures your creativity. Practice mindfulness exercises daily, ensuring you prioritize this sacred time for self-improvement.

You may start with ten minutes each day and gradually increase the duration. Try to be consistent with your timing as well; if you're a morning person, you could use the quiet hours of dawn to practice mindfulness, while night owls may find peace in the tranquility of the moonlit hours.

7.3. Deep Breathing Techniques

Deep breathing is a powerful technique that aligns closely with the principles of mindfulness. It can help calm the mind, reduce anxiety and stress, and foster a conducive environment for your creative flow.

Find a comfortable sitting position, close your eyes, and take a deep breath through your nose, filling your belly with air. Hold this breath for five seconds before exhaling slowly through your mouth. As you breathe out, visualize any negative thoughts, anxiety, or tension leaving your body along with the breath. Do this exercise for at least 10 rounds before starting your work to enhance your focus.

7.4. Mindful Observation

This technique involves thoroughly observing your surroundings to immerse yourself in the present. You make use of your senses – sight, hear, touch, smell – in engaging deeply and genuinely with your environment.

Pick an item nearby and study its details. Notice the texture, the colors, the odor, or even the sound it may make. Details captured through these observations could serve as fresh and unexpected inspirations for your work.

7.5. Walking Meditation

A technique brought to light by Thich Nhat Hanh, Walking Meditation, brings full consciousness to the act of walking. Each step is put in alignment with your breath, creating harmony between your mind, body, and environment.

Choose a distraction-free path. With each step you take, inhale and exhale, synchronizing your footsteps with the rhythm of your breath. All the while, be attentive to your sense of movement, the contact of your feet with the ground, and the subtle feelings in your muscles and joints. This connection with yourself can make you more in tune with building a deeper connection with your art.

7.6. Mindful Eating

Unbelievably, even the act of eating can serve as a mindfulness exercise. Deliberately noticing the texture, taste, and aroma of your food deepens your interest and amplifies your senses, potentially extending these observational skills to your art.

When eating, chew slowly, savoring each bite and its flavor. Try to identify all the individual ingredients, and focus on how the food makes you feel. This exercise enhances your observational and sensory skills.

7.7. Embracing Imperfections

Art isn't about perfection—it's about expression. Being fully present in the moment evicts the anxiety of perfection and paves the way for authenticity. Embrace the idea that there's beauty in imperfections. This act in itself is practicing mindfulness and will aid in pouring your authentic self into your art.

These techniques are not a one-time solution but a continuous journey of practicing and understanding the mind, body, and soul. It may seem laborious initially, but remember that each small step is bringing you closer to boosting your artistic focus. Learn to accept your progress as it comes and avoid rushing the process. With patience and dedication, the ability to channel your focus into your art will become as natural as breathing. Art and mindfulness become unified, each fueling the other in beautiful synergy.

Chapter 8. Embracing Stillness Amidst Chaos: Lessons for Writers

"We have been conditioned to dislike and even fear stillness," says psychotherapist Gary Green. But in this nervous world of ours, the need for tranquility has never been more poignant. The noise of insistent tasks, ever-pulsing social media and personal commitments create a chaotic system that, at first glance, seems impossible to temper. However, it is exactly in these disarrayed moments that the need for stillness becomes critical not only to our state of mind—but to our creativity.

8.1. The Intersection of Stillness and Creativity

Buddha himself was a staunch advocate for stillness, and his teachings reveal an important truth about the universe—that a calm and tranquil mind is where immense creation takes place. Prolific writers and artists throughout history have consistently demonstrated this fact. Virginia Woolf found profound creation in silence and solitude; Beethoven took long, solitary walks amidst nature for his best symphonies, while Albert Einstein claimed he thought best during moments of stillness.

There are scientific explanations corroborating this. In the brain, the Default Mode Network (DMN)—a network that mediates between conscious and unconscious parts of the brain—becomes active during periods of rest. The DMN is responsible for the integration of social, self-referential, and emotional information which causes our most creative ideas to surface.

8.2. Embracing the Quiet

Embracing stillness doesn't mean the absence of movement or becoming a recluse; it simply means reducing external stimulus to help your mind focus on internal thoughts and feelings. In fact, the very nature of stillness is not something that can be grasively defined—it is different for every person.

For one writer, stillness may manifest as early morning sessions of writing in a quiet room with a strong cup of coffee. For an artist, it could be taking daily strolls around the neighborhood, observing the mundanity of life unfold. Stillness exists everywhere—it's in the tranquility of an empty street at dawn, it's in the quiet rustling of leaves, and it's even in the comforting silence shared among close friends. It is these moments of peace that inspire our pens to flow and brushes to paint.

8.3. The Issue of Distractions

In today's digital world, not a moment passes without an onslaught of information. Interruptive notifications from our gadgets, the compulsive need to stay connected and updated, and the looming FOMO (Fear of Missing Out) loom over our concentration, eroding the sanctity of stillness.

Consider this. Turn off the Wi-Fi for an hour, and the torrent of interruptions suddenly stops. Suddenly, the ferocious tempo of life slows down. Ever noticed that? This is the reality of distractions—they feed and proliferate on our attention. The good news? We have the power to control them.

8.4. Drawing Boundaries with Technology

Discipline is the key to preserving your quietude. Make conscious rules about how and when you engage with technology. Set designated 'Quiet Hours' where you put your digital devices on silent or better yet, out of sight. For pathological email checkers, allocate specific times in a day where you can attend to your inbox.

There's no denying the utility of modern technology—it has its role. The caveat lies in preventing it from managing us and our creativity. Moderation is crucial, as with any other aspect of life. By creating boundaries, we can better concentrate on the task at hand and embrace the tranquility often missing in our lives.

8.5. Cultivating a Meditation Practice

Meditation, apart from its multitudinous health benefits, can be a powerful tool in harnessing stillness. Through meditation, we can achieve a calm state of mind that allows us to better tune into our creative juices.

Starting a meditation practice might seem daunting for newbies, but fear not. Begin with a few minutes each day, gradually increasing as you feel more comfortable. You would be amazed at how subtly, yet powerfully, this simple practice can transform your creative processes.

8.6. Conclusion

Embracing stillness amidst chaos can seem like a daunting task. However, remember that chaos and stillness are not at opposite ends of a spectrum, but rather two sides of the same coin. One does not exist without the other, yet it is upon us to choose which side we'd like to look at more often.

Poets, novelists, artists—the masters of creation all have one common thread—proficient at retreating into their inner worlds, they found magic in stillness. If they could do it, so can you. Just remember, stillness is not the end-all-be-all; instead, it's part of a much larger creative venture. It is about acknowledging that tranquility exists within chaos, and that with practice, patience, and mindfulness—you too can find yours.

Chapter 9. Creating Art from Within: The Power of Buddha's Teachings

Breathe in, breathe out. This simple act of mindfulness, derived from the heart of Buddha's teachings, can positively shape the genesis of your artistic creation. But how does one conjure artistry from the depth of mindful breathing? The answer, beloved reader, lies not in the pursuit of the answer itself but in the awakening of one's inner consciousness as you submerge into the teachings of Buddha. Let us journey together deeper into this exploration.

9.1. The Sacred Connection: Mindfulness and Art

The teachings of Buddha elucidate that mindfulness is an integral instrument to attain enlightenment. To succeed in the realm of creativity, an artist must foster a deep connection to their inner self and the world around.

Mindfulness aids in creating this profound connection. When practiced diligently, it delivers an open-minded outlook that adjudicates not the elements of one's environment but purely perceives them. This observation unburdens the mind, akin to a blank canvas ready to be painted afresh.

Let's understand this synergy through some mindful exercises:

Exercise: Observing the world around

1. Find a quiet space.
2. Sit comfortably and close your eyes.

3. Take deep, rhythmic breaths, focusing solely on the act of breathing.

4. Gradually allow your awareness to expand outside your body, to your surroundings.

5. Remind yourself not to judge or interpret what you note. Be an omniscient observer.

Applying this technique in your creative process will refine your perceptions and deepen the soulful expression of your artwork.

9.2. The Crucible of Creativity: Harnessing Mindfulness

Strikingly, the virtues of mindfulness align beautifully with the prerequisites of a potent creative process. Let's explore these interwoven threads:

Focus: Mindfulness sharpens your focus. Just as a sculptor chisels an unformed rock into an exquisite statue, focused attention shapes raw thoughts into polished artistic work.

Openness: Mindfulness esteems present-moment awareness. This awareness mediates revelation, evoking a sense of novelty even in the most mundane places.

Absorption: Buddha's teachings inspire the detachment from one's ego. This detachment facilitates becoming one with the artistic process, further intensifying creative vigor.

These conceptual pillars foster the conditions necessary for your creative subconscious to flourish, thereby nurturing originality in your artistic expressions.

9.3. The Awakened Artist: Enkindling Wisdom through Buddha's Teachings

Buddha's dharma imbues not only a robust armamentarium for mindfulness but also a roadmap towards wisdom. Laminate this wisdom onto your artistic temperament, and the product is an awakened artist, striding gracefully on the path of creativity with an enlightened mind.

The Four Noble Truths: Wisdom begins with acknowledging suffering, its origin, its cessation, and practicing the Noble Eightfold Path to end it. Translate this wisdom into your art; remember that each stroke or word carries a raw emotion, a deeper truth of human existence.

The Noble Eightfold Path: Right understanding, thought, speech, action, livelihood, effort, mindfulness, and concentration serve as guideposts in your creative journey. They aid in maintaining ethical and moral integrity – a commendable asset for any artist.

9.4. The Mindful Art Practice: Translating Buddha's Teachings into Your Art

Now, how do you assimilate these teachings in your artwork? Here are some creative exercises that you can incorporate into your artistic routine:

Exercise: Manifesting Four Noble Truths in Art

1. Reflect on a personal experience of suffering.
2. Express this cathartic encounter through your preferred artistic

medium.

3. Analyze your work: Identify the elements symbolizing the origin and cessation of the suffering.

4. Finally, deduce the depicted Noble Eightfold Path from your creation.

Exercise: Applying the Noble Eightfold Path to Your Creative Process

1. Take a recent artwork or an unfinished project.

2. For each element of the Noble Eightfold Path, note how it's represented or absent within your work.

3. Reflect on these observations, find opportunities for alignment, and implement them in future projects.

With mindful exercises and a thorough immersion into Buddha's teachings, your artistic creations become not merely a mere output of your mind but a soulful depiction of an awakened consciousness. You become not just an artist but a dedicated, mindful creator, etching symbolic narratives and finding dharma in every artistic expression.

In embracing the power of Buddha's teachings to illuminate your artistic journey, you unlock the gateways to a realm of boundless creativity fostered within the comforting lap of mindfulness. The journey might seem long and the path filled with unexplored trails, but remember - you are an artist, a creator who finds beauty in even the most uncharted voyages.

As we end this chapter, pick up your brush, or quill, or instrument, and let the teachings of Buddha inspire your creative soul. In the tranquility of meditation and the awakening of mindfulness, may you find the true essence of your art, blooming in its splendid radiance.

Finally, in the words of Buddha, "Your work is to discover your work and then with all your heart to give yourself to it." – let this be your mantra as you continue your journey within. Remember, within you lies a universe of creativity, it's time to harness it mindfully.

Chapter 10. Incorporating Mindfulness Practices into Your Artistic Routine

Before delving into the world of mindful art, let's take a moment to pause. Close your eyes, focus on your breath, and simply be. Observe the life within you, around you, flowing seamlessly into the universe. As you open your eyes, you are not the same person who closed them a moment ago. You have created art. You have invoked mindfulness.

10.1. Embracing Art and Mindfulness

Art and mindfulness share a beautiful bond, often unnoticed amongst life's continual distractions. Art is creativity in manifest form and mindfulness, an exploration of life's boundless beauty. By intertwining them, what emerges is a splendid tapestry of self-expression, an ode to the present moment's profundities.

Creating art mindfully encourages presence of mind, offering remarkable benefits. It paves the way for better concentration, heightened creativity, and amplified emotional resilience. The union of art and mindfulness isn't just about creating art, but also about infusing every intricate detail and the artistic process with mental and emotional presence.

10.2. Crafting Your Mindful Artistic Routine

The key to incorporating mindfulness in your artistic journey lies in making it a routine, a habit. Start by finding a quiet and well-lit space where you can be uninterrupted. Here are some steps to help structure your mindful art routine:

1. **Set a Clear Intention**: Begin by setting a clear intention about what you want to achieve through your mindful art routine. You might aim to enhance creativity, gain peace of mind, or explore your artistic tendencies. Write it down.

2. **Choose Your Art Medium**: Decide what medium you'd prefer to start your journey with. It might be painting, writing, sculpture, music, or dance. Choose something that speaks to you, something you enjoy.

3. **Set a Schedule**: Like any habit, it requires consistency to make mindfulness a part of your daily life. Set a schedule that fits your lifestyle and stick to it. Begin slowly with 10 minutes a day and gradually increase the time spent.

10.3. Implementing Mindfulness while Creating

As you sit down to create art, turn your focus inwards. You can follow these steps:

1. **Mindful Breathing**: Begin by setting the ambience. Sit comfortably and close your eyes. Focus on your breath, its rhythm, the way it feels as it enters and leaves your body. Incorporate mindful breathing into your routine; it acts as the bridge between your mind and your art.

2. **Mindful Observing**: Open your eyes and begin your art. Notice the materials, their texture, color, and form. Engage your senses fully into the process.

3. **Mindful Creation**: As you create, keep your focus on the strokes, movements, and rhythms of your art. Let each action be purposeful. If your mind starts to wander, gently bring it back.

4. **Art Appreciation**: Post the creative process, spend time appreciating your artwork. Contemplate the art, the process behind it, and how it unfolds stories without words. It isn't about criticizing but appreciating the art born from moments of pure mindfulness.

10.4. Embracing Mistakes as Part of the Process

In creating mindful art, expect the unexpected, for art is rarely flawless. Mistakes, instead of being setbacks, should be stepping stones in your journey. Recognize these not as failures, but as explorations of different paths, roads less travelled by, and relish these surprising detours.

10.5. Mindful Exercises

A well-rounded mindful artistic routine includes various exercises aimed at developing not just the craft, but the person as well. Here are some exercises to incorporate:

1. **Visualizations**: Before starting your artwork, visualize the intended outcome. Visualization encourages the mind to see possibilities, making the creative process smoother.

2. **Journaling**: Maintain a journal of your mindfulness art journey. Highlight the achievements, the challenges, the ideas, and the improvements. Revisit these journals to observe your transformation over time.

3. **Mindful Walks**: Take mindful walks observing your surroundings, gathering inspiration. Engage your senses - sight, hearing, touch, smell, and taste, and let these finds inspire your art.

As you navigate through the steps to incorporate the practice of mindfulness in your art routine, keep in mind that this is a journey. It is not about getting somewhere, but the process itself. Each step, each challenge encountered, each masterpiece created, they form the moments that combine to make this sojourn of mindfulness and art essentially beautiful. Remember, it's the journey that becomes the masterpiece, not just the destination.

Chapter 11. Unleashing Creativity with Buddha-inspired Mindful Meditation

Meditation has been a pillar in Buddhist doctrine for thousands of years, offering adherents a path to peace, insight, and enlightenment. As artists and writers, we can harness this timeless practice to unlock our creative souls and fall into a state of profound creativity. Let's explore this fascinating interplay between mindfulness and creativity drawing upon the wisdom of Buddha, which offers us a novel paradigm shift in our artistic journey.

11.1. Understanding the Concept of Mindfulness in Buddhism

Sati, or mindfulness, is a significant concept in Buddhist philosophy. It implies awareness, attention, and presence—both of mind and body—in each moment. One cultivates mindfulness by engaging in mindful meditation, which typically involves focusing on one's thoughts, sensations, and feelings without passing judgement. This active yet non-reactive attention allows us to dwell fully within the present moment, which is critical for creative practice. Our mind becomes a serene canvas, free of clutter, ready for creative seeds to sprout.

Through mindful meditation, we cultivate a keen understanding of ourselves and our surroundings. This mindfulness forms an empathetic lens through which we view the world—a quality that is critical for the arts. When we nourish this skill, we become more sensitive to life's intricate details, which fosters imagination, inspiration, and innovation.

11.2. The Bridge Between Meditation and Creativity

The mental state achieved during mindful meditation resembles the artistic state of flow—the condition described by psychologist Mihaly Csikszentmihalyi as a space where individuals are completely absorbed in a task, with a sense of joy and effortless action. During such moments, time seems irrelevant, self-consciousness vanishes, and creativity flows freely.

Meditation can, thus, pave the way for this state of flow. It trains us to mould our thoughts, liberating us from being their slaves. Writers can write without self-doubt pestering them, while artists can create without the fear of judgment lurking over them.

11.3. Buddha-Inspired Artistic Practices

Buddha's teachings offer us ways to integrate meditation into our creative processes.

1. **Anapanasati**: Translating to "mindfulness of breathing", this practice teaches us to focus on the natural act of breathing. As we concentrate on our inhale and exhale, we tune out distractions, bringing our attention to the present moment. Artists may find new clarity in their creative vision, while writers may encounter a newfound eloquence in their words.

2. **Metta Meditation**: Also known as loving-kindness meditation, this technique encourages us to cultivate unconditional positive emotions towards all beings. Extending kindness, compassion, and love towards self and others enhances our emotive depth, impacting our artistic creations.

3. **Vipassana Meditation**: This introspective form of meditation

encourages a deep exploration of the self. We observe our thoughts, our feelings, and our actions, without judgment. This method can lead us through insightful self-discoveries, crafting an enriched, authentic narrative for artists and writers alike.

11.4. Harnessing the Power of Mindful Meditation

It's time now to tune into ourselves, relax and let our creativity flourish with these Buddha-inspired mindful tips.

1. **Create a meditation space**: Find a quiet corner, where you can meditate without distractions. It should be comfortable and serene.

2. **Establish a routine**: Set aside a specific time each day for mindful meditation. Consistency will yield better results.

3. **Focus on breath**: To attain mindfulness, start by focusing on your breath, observing each inhale and exhale, the rise and fall of your chest.

4. **Cultivate Metta**: Practice sending out healing affirmations of love and kindness to the universe, then imagine them being reverberated back to you.

5. **Experiment with Vipassana**: Delve into the realms of your inner psyche. Remember, the objective is to observe, not judge.

11.5. Nourishing Creativity Through Mindful Meditation

With disciplined practice and humble patience, mindful meditation can significantly influence your creative abilities. Embrace each moment, word, stroke or note with mindfulness. You'll notice how a simple shift of focus births a ripple of creative prowess within you.

The mind no longer remains a victim of stress, worry or past, but instead becomes the master of the serene present.

As your art frolics within this harmony between the mind and the moment, it resonates with authenticity and depth that naturally spurts from a tranquil mind rooted in the now.

11.6. Concluding Thoughts

Buddha-inspired mindful meditation offers writers and artists a potent way to reignite their creative spark. It does not promise instant success, nor is it a panacea for every artistic hardship. Rather, it is a lifelong journey of discovery—of the self, of our relationship with our art, and of our connection to the universe. And it is in this journey that profound creativity is found.

By undertaking this practice, we begin to see the world—and our place in it—through a new lens. We become more receptive to inspiration and more resilient to setbacks. Our creativity thus becomes a mirror for our mindful state and an emblem of our personal growth. By living and creating mindfully, we give our art a richness, authenticity, and dynamism that can transform our artistic journey.